THE
INFINITE POWER
OF
BELIEF
AND
GRATITUDE

The Two Most Important
Things That Shape Your Life

Brenda Nathan

CONTENTS

Introduction   **5**

WHAT SHAPES YOUR LIFE   **11**

Chapter 1 Your Beliefs   12

Chapter 2 Your State of Mind   19

Chapter 3 Affirmations   29

THE IMPACT THIS HAS ON YOUR LIFE   **41**

Chapter 4 Audit Your Life   42

Chapter 5 Surround Yourself with Positive People   51

Chapter 6 Auditing Your Time   55

Chapter 7 Self-Care Is a Must   60

Chapter 8 You Are Enough   66

YOU ARE MEANT FOR MORE   **72**

Chapter 9 You Have a Bigger Purpose   73

Chapter 10 Your Identity   79

Chapter 11 Giving   85

KEEP THE MOMENTUM   **90**

Chapter 12 Keep Moving Forward   91

Chapter 13 Create Your Reality   99

Chapter 14 Decide and Commit   106

Chapter 15 Gratitude Practice   111

Conclusion   **117**

Acknowledgements   **123**

INTRODUCTION
My Road to Gratitude

I t's amazing what people can do when they believe in something. Some people climb Mount Kilimanjaro. Some people learn many languages. Me? Since I was a child, I've been using the concept of St. Anthony to find my lost socks.

When I was seven years old, my mother took me on vacation to the seaside. The weather was not good. The ocean was covered by such a thick layer of fog that we had difficulty seeing through it, but out to sea was a statue of St. Anthony that I could just make out.

As we gazed at the statue, my mother said, "St. Anthony is good for lost things." She was a schoolteacher and often liked to impart such nuggets of information to me.

"You mean if you lose something, you can get it back by asking St. Anthony?" I asked.

"Yes," she said, still gazing out at the sea. She was lost in her thoughts, and we stood looking silently for a while, until it started to drizzle and we returned to the house.

From then on, I found my lost things by asking St. Anthony. I never questioned it. If I lost my earring, I would ask, walk towards the place it had dropped, and I'd find it. Easy.

As I got older, I realized that other people did not find their lost possessions this way, even my own family. I was the only person in my house able to find lost things. Why didn't they ask St. Anthony, I wondered, like my mother had taught me? It was so easy.

One day, I lost a really high-value gift card when we were moving house. My brother said he had put it in a drawer before the movers took the piece of furniture to the new house. We looked inside the drawer, searched through all the boxes, and hunted everywhere else in the house. We couldn't find it.

I knew I couldn't ask St. Anthony for help at that moment; I had to be in the right state of mind to ask.

I was too angry with my brother for putting it in the drawer instead of giving it to me.

I closed my eyes. "I like this house," I said to myself. "I like my brother. I'm fine." I kept repeating these words for a few minutes. I felt my affirmations working, and I began to calm. I asked St. Anthony, "Where is the gift card?"

I walked towards the drawer. I could sense it, in between two side drawers, but I couldn't see it. I felt around between the drawers . . . and pulled the gift card out.

I always feel amazed when I receive something after asking St. Anthony, no matter how often I do it. And I always say thank you to St. Anthony.

When my brother came back, I told him I had found the gift card inside the drawer. "Are you kidding me?" he asked. He had looked for it in the same drawer several times. He commented on how good I am at finding things in the house.

After this incident, I approached this topic with my mother. "Mom, St. Anthony is good for lost things, right?"

"Yes," she replied. "St. Anthony is good for lost things. When fishermen go out to sea, if they become lost, they ask St. Anthony to guide them, and then they find their way home."

I froze. "You mean it's for fishermen?" I asked.

"Yes, when they are lost at sea," my mother replied.

I was stunned. "Not for finding anything else?"

"Yes," she said again, looking at me strangely. "Just fishermen."

"But I thought . . . I thought when you said lost things . . . if we lost something, we ask St. Anthony and get it back."

"No," she replied. "Not unless you're a fisherman."

I'd been asking St. Anthony for years to find my lost things and never realized that he was not for meant for me.

But this didn't stop me. I continued to do it as I always had, and I never lost my knack for finding things.

***

What is your knack?

According to the dictionary, a knack is an acquired or natural skill at performing a task.

But I define it differently. To me, a knack is something that comes naturally to you in a way that it doesn't to other people.

Everyone has knacks. You may think your knack is not very useful, or you might think that anyone can do it. They take many different forms. People can do voices, write backwards, find wayward coins on the ground, read minds, draw faces, remember phone numbers, contort their bodies in strange ways, create stunning floral arrangements, make a perfect dish, and do other fun or unusual things.

They are indications of how powerful you can be when you allow things to happen, when you expect that something will happen, and when you are in the right state of mind.

Your natural state of mind is feeling gratitude, appreciation, curiosity, excitement, and joy. This is called your flow state. It is in this state that you can do anything you want without doubting yourself. You just get on with doing it. When you believe in what you're doing and you are in your flow state, everything is possible.

You are also in your flow state when you are fully immersed in doing something that you enjoy and love. In this state, you often lose track of time and feel energized.

I will discuss in later chapters how the two most important things that shape your life are your beliefs and your state of mind. But for now, take five minutes to think about your knack . . .

What is your knack? What is your belief behind this knack? Where did you get this belief?

WHAT
SHAPES
YOUR LIFE

Chapter 1

YOUR BELIEFS

B elief is the acceptance that something is true. Your beliefs start in childhood, and you develop more beliefs as you grow up. You pick up beliefs from family, friends, teachers, spouses, significant others, coworkers—anyone you interact with. Beliefs are a part of your subconscious and, unless you become consciously aware of them, you continue to act on them subconsciously.

Beliefs are self-fulfilling. When you believe something, you also manifest it. You receive what you believe.

If you believe you don't have time for exercise, you will fill your time with things that do not leave you time to exercise. If you believe you can never win, you will continue to do things that cause you to lose. If you believe it is too late for you, you will remain stuck in place, unmoving.

Negative and Positive Beliefs

There are negative beliefs and positive beliefs. Here are some examples:

Negative beliefs	Positive beliefs
1. I can never do this	1. I can do anything
2. I don't have time	2. I have time to do what I love
3. I don't have experience	3. I have experience in things that matter to me
4. I am slow	4. I go at my own pace
5. It's too late for me	5. I am powerful
6. I can never win	6. I can find the way
7. I am alone	7. I can connect to my spirituality
8. I am not qualified	8. I am called to do this
9. No one can help me	9. I am capable
10. I don't know enough	10. I am capable of learning

Question Your Negative Beliefs

Your beliefs are what create your experience. If you believe something is possible, without questioning and doubting it, then you will make it happen. Therefore, you <u>must</u> question every negative belief you hold. You have the power to create a new belief whenever you want, which means that you can consciously change your negative belief to a positive belief.

When you have a belief like "*I am a failure*" or "*No one can help me,*" you must investigate this belief, even if it feels very real to you. Ask yourself two questions:

(1) Are the thoughts I'm thinking true?

(2) Where did this belief come from?

Let's take an example. Suppose you believe that *you are a failure.*

Question 1 – Are the thoughts I'm thinking true?

Write down the area or areas where you think you have failed. Then write down areas of your life that you are succeeding in.

Be specific with your answers when you are investigating your belief.

Think of the times you have succeeded in the past and write them down on a piece of paper. Count the small wins, even going back to childhood.

Question 2 – Where did this belief come from?

Who gave you the belief that you must succeed all the time and in every area of your life? Maybe some of the failures on your list have led to successes that you've also listed. Failing in a single instance doesn't mean you will fail in the future. Perhaps you didn't have the right tools and you didn't succeed then, but you can now find new tools to have success in future attempts.

Maybe your business failed, but you take good care of your body. Maybe you don't have good friends, but you volunteer in the community.

The quickest way to change your negative beliefs to positive beliefs is to change them to the opposite of what they were. Shift your negative belief of "*I am a failure*" to "*I am a winner*" or "*I am successful in areas that I focus on.*" Write down your new positive belief.

Sharing Your Beliefs

You can consciously create a new positive belief whenever you want. However, you should be careful about who you share these new beliefs with.

You are sitting with a group of friends, and you have changed your negative belief from "*I am not smart,*" to "*I am a genius!*" You say to them, "*I'm a genius.*" What's the first thing they tell you?

Do they say, "*Absolutely, you are a genius!*"? Or do they laugh because they think you're making a joke? Or might they say, "*Please, just be real.*"?

You *are* a genius, inside and out. You have things that you are good at and love to do. And yet, if you tell someone you are a genius, they will find it strange or amusing because you are judged and measured by other peoples' ideas of what constitutes a genius. We live in a world where saying good things about ourselves seems boastful. This creates a pattern where you continue undermining yourself until you start believing the absurd lie that you are not smart or beautiful or that you are a failure, when this isn't true at all.

Ignore the negativity and seek feedback from positive people, especially in the early stages when you are working to change your negative beliefs to positive beliefs.

You Get What You Believe

Everything you need to live your best life, a life of joy, well-being, fulfilment, and freedom, is within you. You get what you believe.

Beliefs are self-fulfilling. You get what you believe.

Summary: Your Beliefs

1) Belief is the acceptance that something is true.

2) There are positive and negative beliefs.

3) Question and investigate your negative beliefs and change them to positive beliefs.

4) Be careful who you share your new beliefs with.

5) Believe that everything you need to live your best life is within you. You get what you believe.

Homework

Think of five negative beliefs you have that are holding you back. How can you change those to positive beliefs?

Chapter 2

YOUR STATE OF MIND

Managing the emotional state you are in is the most important thing you can do for yourself.

How are you feeling right now? Are you feeling excited? Are you curious? Are you joyful? Are you feeling alive? Are you appreciating everything around you?

Take a moment to think on this now. Appreciate all the things and experiences. Good, bad, however you define it; appreciate all of it. Feelings of gratitude, appreciation, joy, creativity, happiness, excitement, playfulness, and curiosity are a state of mind. They are energy-charging emotions. You feel good when you feel these emotions. These are also your natural flow state.

Your natural flow state is soil, the fertile soil that is necessary for the plant (you) to grow. Without fertile soil, the plant cannot grow. You cannot grow.

In this natural flow state, you become a loving human being, you connect to your surroundings, and you make good decisions in areas that matter to you—such as health, relationships, family, career, personal growth, contribution, and spirituality.

Energy-Draining and Energy-Charging Emotions

Energy-draining emotions include feeling angry, sad, overwhelmed, helpless, numb, and worried. These emotions sap energy from you. In this state, a person is thinking over and over about something that is not working well for them. In this state, you feel tired, unhappy and may procrastinate.

Energy-charging emotions include love, excitement, aliveness, gratitude, appreciation, confidence, interest, and stimulation. These emotions give you an energy boost. In this state, you feel happy, connected, and productive.

Energy-charging emotions	Energy-draining emotions
Excited, curious, alive, appreciated, grateful, loved, passionate, amused, calm, capable, caring, confident, relaxed, happy, inspired, trusting, enthusiastic, attractive, connected, content, interested, stimulated	Angry, sad, helpless, worried, frustrated, resentment, jealous, arrogant, disgusted, annoyed, frightened, disappointed, ashamed, nasty, rejected, shattered, inadequate, aggressive, upset, enraged, humiliated

How to Change Your State Instantly

The trick to instantly changing your state is through repeating positive affirmations to yourself. Affirmations are words that you consciously choose to say. When you repeat affirmations, they become imprinted in your subconscious mind. When you think and say positive words, this makes you feel calm and good inside. Suppose you say, *"Everything is happening perfectly for me"* or *"This moment is perfect for me."* It is difficult to feel negatively when uttering these words. Affirmations are an important topic and I have devoted a full chapter (3) to them. For now, I want you to remember that the quickest way to change your state is to repeat positive affirmations to yourself.

Dealing with Worries

One of the biggest energy-draining emotions you feel is that of general worries.

Worries are fears in disguise: the fear of something that may or may not happen in the future. You fear that if the situation happened to you, you could not handle it. It begins to overwhelm you and you feel helpless because you cannot control the outcome.

Worrying is almost always pointless, at least often enough that it's not worth doing. Some pointless worries include fears about the past affecting your future, worry for the well-being of loved ones, economy, being rejected, what other people think of you, whether you are good enough, how you look, or making a mistake.

You may have a "What if this happens?" worry, such as "*What if this happened to my loved ones?*" or "*What if there is an accident?*" There is also another common type of worry, "Should I do this or should I not?" "*Should I leave this job or not?*" "*Should I ask her on a date or not?*" "*Should I ask my boss for a pay raise or not?*" "*Should I make a call or not?*"

Worries that can be acted on need your attention. The more you delay that action, the more time you spend pointlessly worrying. For worries that don't need your immediate action, I have a tool that ensures you're not spending negative energy on them while they're not relevant to your life. This is called postponing. Here is how postponing your worry works.

Step 1 – Postpone Your Worry to Next Week

When a worry comes into your mind, put it aside. Say to yourself, "I'm postponing (state the worry) to next week."

When next week comes, you probably won't remember this worry. If you do, simply postpone the worry to next week again.

If there is a worry that is persisting despite using this statement, use a future date to postpone it. Every time you think about what concerns you, think, "I am not worrying about this until Tuesday, and today is not Tuesday."

Postponing removes the feeling of helplessness and of being overwhelmed. When you postpone your worry to next week, it clears your mind of this clutter. If it is a worry about the future that you have no control over, keep postponing this worry until it no longer overwhelms you!

Some worries can be persistent and overwhelming. Something may have happened to you in the past that changed the trajectory of your life, such as a serious illness, divorce, business failure, relationship breakup, or the loss of a loved one. Maybe you thought your life was going to be one way and something happened that completely changed the direction of your life. In a situation like this, you are in a new place with an uncertain future. You may feel isolated. You are not alone in experiencing this, but worrying about the future will only overpower you. Postpone even this persistent worry about the future until next week.

Step 2 – You Can Handle It

Say these words aloud: "Whatever happens, I can handle it."

When the time comes, you are capable of facing anything!

Think of a time in your life when you handled a difficult experience, such as the loss of a job, a relationship break-up, a health issue, a family issue, or money troubles.

Do you recall the sense of achievement once it was over and handled? There is always something you can think from the past that may have worried you at the time, but once it happened, you just handled it. Worry overwhelms you and keeps you stuck. Worries steal the life that you have right now in this moment.

Step 3 – Feel Excited to Live in This Moment

When you postpone your worry and acknowledge that you can handle anything, you need to find something else to focus on. Worry clutters your mind and takes a lot of space—now you can fill the "no worry moment" you have created, to feel excitement, appreciation, curiosity, and joy. You can use this space that the worry had occupied to try something new. It doesn't need to be big. Start small. Look for something new to do every day. Expand your comfort zone; feel the excitement that comes with living in the moment. Take a new route to work, cook a new dish, write a message to a friend, work on a new project. Get excited and be enthusiastic. Soon you will find you have discarded your worry and replaced it with much more exciting activities.

Gratitude and Intention

There is intention behind everything that you do in your life, whether you know it or not. Become aware of your thoughts. Choose to experience your life consciously all the time in a state of gratitude, appreciation, love, curiosity, happiness, and joy.

Being grateful every day does not mean you have to do or achieve big things every day. Instead focus on the average things that you take for granted, like electricity, technology, food, the breath in your lungs, the roof over your head, the clothes you wear, your supportive family and friends, a comfortable bed, your phone, the books you read, and your good health.

Positive emotions come to you when you are active. Move your body. Smile, laugh, sing, dance, walk, run. You don't need a reason to smile–smile anyway! You don't need a reason to laugh. Just laugh out loud. You don't need to have a perfect voice to sing. Sing as loud as you want to. Create your own happiness. Get excited to live your life.

Managing

the state

you are in

is the most

important thing

you can do

for yourself.

Summary: Your State of Mind

1) Gratitude, appreciation, joy, and curiosity are all energy-charging emotions. You feel good when you feel these emotions.

2) When you feel angry, sad, overwhelmed, helpless, or numb, you are experiencing energy-draining emotions. These sap energy from you.

3) You can change your emotional state instantly by repeating positive affirmations.

4) Worry clutters your mind and takes up a lot of space. If something needs action, take that action. Otherwise, postpone your worries to next week.

5) Feel excited to live in this moment.

Homework

1) Name one worry that you are currently experiencing.

2) If something needs your action, take that action.

3) Otherwise, postpone that worry to next week.

4) If the worry comes back, keep postponing it to next week.

Chapter 3

AFFIRMATIONS

The quickest way to change your emotional state is through affirmations. Affirmations are so powerful that the basics of your life can remain the same, but by repeating these affirmations, things will slowly start to change for the better.

Affirmations are positive statements that you consciously choose to say. When you think and say these words, it makes you feel good inside. Suppose you say, "*I am getting better and better every day.*" It is not easy to feel negative emotions when uttering these words. However, you need to believe in the statements you say. If you choose a positive affirmation but you don't feel it is true, you will negate the positive aspect.

You need to align the positive statements with your internal feelings.

"*I am exercising regularly, and it is helping me reach my ideal weight*," is more powerful than just, "*I am exercising regularly*."

Affirmations need to be in the present tense. Use words such as *am* and *have* and avoid the word *will*. Affirmations can refer to what you have or what you would like to have.

Affirmations can reprogram your mind into believing that the words you say are true. If you repeat an affirmation enough times, *it will become your belief*. If you keep repeating the statement "*I am always with the wrong people*," you will believe that this is true and you will attract people who don't serve your higher purpose.

Negative and Positive Affirmations

When you are feeling negative emotions, you tend to repeat negative affirmations. Most of the time, you don't even notice the negative affirmations that you are repeating to yourself. Some negative affirmations are:

I am a mess

I could never get this right

I hate my job

I don't have good friends

I am always with the wrong people

I hate my life

He (or She) destroyed me

I feel lousy

I don't have a choice

I am a pain

People don't value my opinion now

My productivity level is low

Everything has gone wrong

I always eat the wrong food

I have too many problems

I am helpless

It's too difficult

I can never change

I don't have money

I have never really laughed

I am not going to make it

I am stuck

I can't do this anymore

I am getting old

These negative affirmations disempower you. Even if some of these are true, such as "*I don't have good friends*," saying these words only reinforces the very thing that you currently don't want in your life. The statement "*I don't have good friends*" will soon turn into the belief, "*I will never have good friends*" and will not help you change this situation. Change your negative affirmations to positive affirmations such as "*I am a great friend and there are great people out there coming into my life.*"

Positive affirmations empower you. Some positive affirmations are:

I am enjoying living this wonderful life

I surround myself with people who empower me

My life is amazing

I accept myself as I am

Today is a new beginning for me

I am attracting abundance in all areas of my life

I am amazing

I can handle it

I listen to my gut

I am a loving person

I am beautiful

I am having fun

I am a genius

I accept it as it is

My life is full of joy

I am living my life

I feel awesome

I am taking care of my body by doing …

I love you … (say your name after these words)

I am committed to taking action everyday

I am creating my destiny

I am unstoppable

I am a hero

I live in the now

It is a beautiful world

It is a privilege to live in this world

I choose where I want to go

I choose who I want to spend time with

I choose what I want to feel

I choose what I want in life

I am living my life with purpose

I am happy to serve others

I contribute to my fellow human beings

I am investing my time into my personal growth

I am wired for success

I appreciate everything around me

I am perfect inside and out

I am willing to learn

I am getting healthier and healthier every day

Specific Positive Affirmations

Your positive affirmations can even be specific to your goals—relationship, family, health, success, career, personal development, spirituality.

Affirmations for Health and Wellness:

I am healthy and feel great in every inch of my body.

I enjoy eating healthy food, and it is helping me attain my ideal weight.

I nourish my body with fuel that gives me strength and love.

I have loads of energy and I am living my purpose.

Affirmations for Love:

I am attracting the love of my life and my life is full of joy.

I am happy to have this special bond with my partner and enjoy their company.

Affirmations for Career and Business:

My job is my passion and I love doing what I do.

Business opportunities are coming my way and I get to live the life I love.

Affirmations for Abundance:

All my needs are satisfied right now and I am enjoying this journey of life.

I am open to limitless possibilities and am living my life on my terms.

General Purpose Affirmations:

I am powerful and all I need is within me.

I am enough and everything is happening perfectly for me.

Repeating Affirmations

A technique you can use when repeating affirmations to make you feel them more strongly is to stress the words differently every time you say them.

If your affirmation is:

My happiness comes from within me.

You can repeat this affirmation as follows stressing the words differently every time.

<u>MY</u> happiness comes from within me.

My <u>HAPPINESS</u> comes from within me.

My happiness <u>COMES</u> from within me.

My happiness comes <u>FROM</u> within me.

My happiness comes from <u>WITHIN</u> me.

My happiness comes from within <u>ME</u>.

Your Positive Affirmations

Write down your positive affirmations and repeat them over and over. Really mean it.

Feel the emotion. You can say them out loud while doing your daily activities like taking a shower, driving, walking, doing laundry, cleaning, and preparing meals. Moving your body while repeating your affirmations makes them more powerful.

Become aware when you are saying negative affirmations to yourself. Stop and change them to positive affirmations immediately. Awareness is the first step, so don't beat yourself up if you realize you are saying a negative affirmation. Stop and change it.

Affirmations, Belief, and State of Mind

You repeat affirmations that turn into your beliefs, which then affects the emotional state you are in, and vice versa.

Suppose you repeat the words "*I am a loser*," "*I tend to always do the wrong things,*" "*Bad things always happen to me.*" This will turn into the negative belief, "*I am not lucky.*" Which will then make you angry and sad which is a negative state.

Let's see this example work in the other direction. You feel angry and sad because something bad happened. Then you start repeating affirmations to yourself: "*I am a loser,*" "*I tend to always do the wrong things,*" and "*Bad things always happen to me.*" The more you repeat this to yourself, the more this will become your belief: "*I am not lucky.*"

The state you are in influences the emotions you are feeling and the statements you are repeating to yourself, and this eventually becomes your belief.

Change Your Affirmations

Suppose you consciously change the negative belief "*I am not lucky*" to a positive belief: "*I am resourceful, and I always find a way.*" Then you start repeating affirmations that are consistent with this belief – "*I am unstoppable,*"

"I am the creator of my life," *"I choose what I want in my life."* This makes you feel excited and confident. Luck will find its way to you!

You have the choice to consciously change your belief or state of mind anytime you want. You can do this by repeating positive affirmations.

The quickest
way to change
your state
is through
repeating
affirmations.

Summary: Affirmations

1) The quickest way to change your emotional state is through affirmations.

2) If you repeat affirmations enough times, it will become your belief.

3) There are negative and positive affirmations.

4) Become aware of the affirmations you are repeating to yourself.

5) Change your negative affirmations to positive affirmations and repeat these over and over with emotion.

Homework

Write down three negative affirmations you tend to repeat regularly. Change them to positive affirmations now. Say them aloud and repeat these positive affirmations over and over every day for the next 30 days.

THE IMPACT THIS HAS ON YOUR LIFE

Chapter 4

AUDIT YOUR LIFE

D o a review of your life. Examine every facet. Are you living your best life?

Tell yourself the truth. Where are you right now? Do you wish things were different? Do you wish you were surrounded by different people? Wishing can help you identify what you want, but the act of wishing is a waste of time. The only way you are going to grow and be the person you want to be is to be brutally honest with yourself at all times.

You must take the first step in creating the life you want. Wishing things were different is not going to serve your purpose. You must design your life the way you want it to be. When you move out of your comfort zone, you are going to make mistakes. That does not mean you should stay where you are.

Most of the time, you aren't honest with yourself and just hope that others don't notice it. You project an image that is the opposite of what is really going on in your life. Many times, you are trying to be everything to everyone and forget who you really are. Tell yourself the truth so that you can make shifts to a more meaningful and purposeful life.

(1) Where Are You Right Now?

Rate these aspects of your life from 1-10, with 10 being absolute fulfilment, energy, and vitality to 1 being low energy and no fulfilment. Be brutally honest.

Where are you currently in the following areas:

Health

Relationship

Career

Finances

Family & friends

Personal growth

Time management

Spirituality

Contribution

You can also choose your own areas. The above are only a few aspects that I have selected.

If you have assigned a 10 to any of these areas, ask yourself this question: Do I not want to grow and make any improvements in this area? Human beings need to keep learning and growing, otherwise we will feel stuck and bored. If you rate your career as a 10, is there not any area you can improve in your career? Then rate it lower and make those improvements. There is always a next level up for every area. Rate these honestly and find ways to take them to the next level.

You are exactly where you are meant to be. Every area of your life is a direct reflection of your past conditioning. Do not pass judgement on yourself or beat yourself up. Today is a starting point for you.

(2) What Do You Want?

Once you know where you are, your next step is to know what you want. Write it down.

What does your best life look like? What does it feel like? What do you want your life to feel like in all these areas? Don't worry about how you are going to achieve it just yet. This is about your best life, your ideal life.

What do you want the following areas to be like?

Health

Relationship

Career

Finances

Family & friends

Personal growth

Time management

Spirituality

Contribution

(3) **Why Do You Want It?**

Knowing your "why" is important as this is what will drive you forward when you have setbacks.

You might want to have more energy, feel healthy and alive, find a great relationship, grow more spiritual, start a new business, have financial freedom, spend more time with family, make new friends. You need to be clear on why you need to improve the areas you have listed. What do you see as the benefits of making these improvements?

Write down your why.

(4) Investigate Your Beliefs and Make Small Changes

To move from where you are now to where you want to be, you need to examine your current beliefs in these areas. This is an important process and should not be skipped. You must change the belief that is holding you back in areas you want to improve before you take the small changes towards the life you want.

Follow these three steps to change your belief for each area that you want to improve:

Step1: Investigate your current belief

If your current situation is that you have money problems and you want to have financial independence, jot down your current beliefs about money. Someone who has a belief "*You need money to make money,*" or "*I can never make more money,*" or "*I am not good with money,*" will continue not to create wealth in their life.

Step 2: Change your current belief

Create a new belief about money. These beliefs must be not in the future but in the present. Don't create a belief such as "*I will make money.*" Instead, a new belief can be something like, "*I am resourceful, and I can find a way to make money,*" or "*money flows easily into my life,*" or "*I attract money easily and money changes things.*"

Step 3: Schedule your time every day to make small changes

Make small changes towards where you want to be. In the example above about money, start to list your spending as a first step or list possible new ways to make extra money. If you want to make a small shift in health, start moving your body for 5 minutes today and increase by 1 more minute tomorrow.

Schedule your time to make these shifts. Put it in your calendar and block that time for it. Make sure these are small shifts that you can make easily. Don't set yourself up to fail in these early steps. If you keep postponing these shifts, then look at them again and make the shifts even smaller so that you can easily do them.

Work on the small shifts now because a small seed that you plant today will grow into a big tree in the future. But you must nurture it. Take care of the soil, water it, and keep believing.

Shape Your Life

We human beings must keep growing. By always telling yourself the truth, changing your beliefs, and making small shifts, you can achieve a high level of personal growth and a life of meaning and purpose.

Hold yourself accountable for making these shifts and create momentum. Don't hide behind wishful thinking. You can choose to see the world with all its blemishes and chart your path in a way that addresses all your difficulties head-on. In this way, you can achieve anything that you desire.

Where are you now?

Investigate and
change your belief.

Make small shift towards
where you want to be.

Summary: Audit Your Life

1) With brutal honesty, write down where you are in each area of your life.

2) Write down what you want these areas to look like for your best life.

3) Write down why you want it.

4) Investigate your current beliefs in each area and make small shifts towards your best life.

5) Hold yourself accountable for making these small shifts and create momentum.

Homework

Read aloud the answers you have written down on where you are in each area of your life, where you want to be, and your why.

Investigate your current belief about one area, change it to a positive belief, and act on a small shift today.

Chapter 5

SURROUND YOURSELF WITH POSITIVE PEOPLE

Here is a concept to ponder: you are the average of the five people you spend the most time with. Whatever you want to achieve in life and whatever you want to become, you must focus on cultivating an environment that will get you there, and that environment is going to be composed of the people you choose to include in your life. If you surround yourself with positive, healthy, successful people, you will greatly enhance your own chances of achieving positivity, health, and abundance.

Surround yourself with positive people. Negativity drives negativity.

Who you surround yourself with influences your emotional state. Negativity is a virus that worms its way into your world and spreads quickly into all areas of your life. After some time, it weighs you down so much that you lose energy and vitality and it begins to affect your body.

You want to be part of a circle of friends and family that lifts those around them. But you only need one negative person in a group to infect everyone.

If people around you are angry or upset, become aware of it and don't join them in their negativity. Stay in your place of positivity and peace.

You need to be challenged, encouraged, and supported by people around you. When you seek advice from those around you, make sure that their intention is what is best for you and not what is best for them.

It is important to choose your confidants carefully. The people with whom you spend the most time are going to impact your life.

Who you surround yourself with is who you become.

Who you
surround
yourself with
is who you
become.

Summary: Surround Yourself with Positive People

1) Carefully choose the people who you spend most of your time with. Negativity drives negativity.

2) Who you surround yourself with influences your emotional state.

3) Become aware and don't join in other people's negativity.

4) You need to be challenged, encouraged, and supported by people around you.

5) Who you surround yourself with is who you become.

Homework

Think of the five people you spend the most time with. How are they impacting your life?

Chapter 6

AUDITING YOUR TIME

There is a limited amount of time available to you. If today was your last day on this earth, how would you spend it? Who would you spend your time with? What would you spend your time doing?

Audit your time for a week. Track your time by writing down everything you are spending your time on in 30-minute intervals. You can then read back through them, analyzing how you are spending your time and working out whether you are living life to the fullest and making the most of your time.

If you are watching the news, complaining, spending time with negative people, checking emails every minute, spending unnecessary time on chats, gossiping and excessively browsing the internet, then you are not using your time effectively and it's very likely that it is negatively influencing your emotional state.

How you spend your time influences the emotional state you are in.

Don't wait for the perfect time to start something new. Don't wait for the perfect time to say "I love you" to a loved one.

Say "No"

Regrets in life come from not spending time with who you truly love, or not doing things that truly fulfil you. When you audit your time, pick areas that you can say "no" to so that you spend your time on the things that you *do* want to do.

Create a "Do Not Do List"

Keep a "Do not do" list and follow through so that you are not spending your time on things that are not important to you. When you find yourself doing things on the "Do not do list," stop immediately.

Schedule Your Time

You may take the people around you for granted, and don't spend enough time with them. Schedule time to spend with your loved ones. Block time in your calendar. To find the time, you may need to say "no" to a lot of things that are not serving your purpose.

Don't put off things that need doing. Schedule time to spend on areas of your life that need improvement. The small shifts that may need to be made include areas of health, relationship, family, career, business, friendship, personal growth, spirituality, and general contribution to a life of meaning and purpose. When you consciously schedule your time, you make small shifts that will create a big difference in your life.

Use Your Time Effectively

How you use your time influences the emotional state you are in and determines the quality of your life.

Say no

to things

that don't

serve your

purpose.

Summary: Auditing Your Time

1) Audit your time. Track your time by writing down everything you are spending your time on in 30-minute intervals.

2) Pick areas that you can say "no" to so that you are free to spend your time on things that you *do* want to do.

3) Keep a "Do not do" list.

4) Consciously schedule and block your time every day for things that serve your purpose.

5) How you use your time determines the quality of your life.

Homework

Audit your time for a week. Write down everything you are spending your time on.

Pick three things that you are currently spending time on that are not important to you and include them on your "Do not do list."

Chapter 7

SELF-CARE IS A MUST

Taking care of yourself emotionally, physically, and spiritually is the biggest gift you can give yourself and the loved ones around you. You must take care of yourself before you can take care of everyone else.

Taking care of yourself is not selfish. You give love to others when you take care of yourself because if you do not take care of yourself, you are expecting someone else to take care of you. Self-care is 100% your responsibility.

Take Care of Your Mind and Body

Feed your mind with positive things. Spend at least 30 minutes a day reading a book or listening to an audiobook or podcast on positivity. You can listen to an audiobook while doing other tasks such as walking, cooking, doing laundry, exercising, commuting to work, or driving.

Take care of your body. Pay attention to what you are putting into your body. If you don't feel good when you eat or drink something, make a decision to change it.

Move your body. Spend at least 30 minutes a day exercising. Some great activities include walking, running, or yoga. When you move your body, you feel good. Moving your body changes your emotional state. If you are upset about something, you will feel better if you go for a walk. If you combine moving your body with repeating positive affirmations, then you will truly transform your experience.

Your body stays with you till the end of your life. Take good care of it.

Repeat this affirmation:

I give love to myself and others when I take care of my mind and body.

Love Yourself

Love yourself. Be kind to yourself. Believe in yourself. You are loved as you are.

Never give up on yourself. We are more ready to pick others up than ourselves. Give yourself the love that you would give to others. That is true love. You cannot love another if you don't love yourself.

Don't postpone your happiness. Enjoy your life right now.

Morning Routine

What is your morning routine?

Don't check your phone as soon as you wake up or whenever you wake up during the night. Cultivate a morning routine that empowers you for the day.

Don't set an alarm and then keep pushing the snooze button. When you push the snooze button, this tells your mind that your precious day is not important. Set the exact time you need to wake up and get up as soon as your alarm goes off. Do this no matter how tired you are or how few hours of sleep you have had. Make it a habit to never push the snooze button.

Each morning, say one or two things that you are grateful for. Maybe you're grateful to be alive!

Move your body or do physical activity for least 5 minutes in the morning. This could be stretching your body or going for a short walk. Moving your body creates a good feeling. Why not start every day feeling good?

Take care of your mind. Be aware of the emotional state you are in. You are going to have lapses in your positive state. Things happen that you don't have control of. When you become aware of an unhappy state, celebrate your awareness, and don't beat yourself up. Being aware of your emotional state means that you can now change your unhappy state to a positive one through using positive affirmations. Say these positive affirmations out loud until you feel your emotional state change.

Different options for morning routines include meditation, yoga, gratitude journaling, repeating affirmations, reading, moving your body, singing, scheduling the day, thinking of the wins that you had the day before, etc. Pick something that makes you feel great!

Here is a simple and quick morning routine:

1) Do not look at your phone as soon as you wake up.

2) Repeat positive affirmations. You can repeat these affirmations while you make your bed.

3) Notice something you are grateful for and say it.

4) Move your body for 5 minutes.

You give love
to yourself and
others when you
take care of your
mind and body.

Summary: Self-Care Is a Must

1) Taking care of yourself is the biggest gift you can give yourself and the people around you.

2) Move your body. Spend at least 30 minutes a day doing some sort of movement-based activity.

3) Feed your mind with positive things. Spend at least 30 minutes a day reading a book or listening to an audiobook or podcast that provides a source of positivity.

4) Love yourself. Be kind to yourself. Believe in yourself. You are loved as you are.

5) Cultivate a morning routine that empowers you for the day.

Homework

Start tomorrow with a simple and quick morning routine that empowers you for the day.

Chapter 8

YOU ARE ENOUGH

N o one in their true nature is angry or jealous. These qualities only develop when you identify yourself with ego. Ego is a delusion that you are not enough. You must get out of your delusion. When you love yourself and others, you are in your true natural state.

You are loved as you are. Be you. You are enough.

Be Authentic

Being authentic means that you behave exactly as you are. You don't concern yourself with what other people are thinking. Other people's thoughts are not really about you; their opinion of you is just a reflection of what is happening in their life.

Be curious about your experiences. You don't know all the answers; you can only guess. Open your mind to all of the possibilities in this world. Don't be tied to other people's opinions or judgements. Let your inner self guide you. You are created perfectly. In fact, you're kind of a big deal.

You are enough when you are authentic.

Perfection

When you set a goal, you decide what perfection means for you and then you beat yourself up for not achieving it. Perfection stops you from becoming who you are meant to become. It gives you an excuse to do nothing for fear of failing to meet that standard.

When you believe everything is happening perfectly for you, that is how you will experience it.

Don't get stuck with perfection.

Don't Beat Yourself Up

Things are going to happen that you have no control over. Regrets happen. Decisions are made based on the information you have at that time, which isn't always perfect or even correct. Don't waste time wishing your past was different. Regardless of whether it is something you've done, something you haven't done, or something someone has done or not done to you, the past is past. Mistakes happen. That's called living. Keep moving forward.

Let Go

How often have you fallen into a trap set by your own mind? You become convinced that happiness is something you need to put a lot of effort into rather than something you can simply accept. Satisfaction and joy are always within your reach because they are your natural state. You need to let go of the markers and judgment lines that you have set for yourself.

Don't judge yourself or others. Accept others exactly as they are. It is the biggest gift you can give someone. You cannot connect with someone properly if you are judging them. Appreciate and understand others' worlds and the lenses through which they are viewing them.

You are also using filters based on your own understanding. Be kind to yourself too. The most important thing is for you to stay in a positive state no matter what happens around you.

When you worry about other people judging you, is it possible you are also judging yourself? Stop living in a state of judgment. Change your state to one of positivity. Be kind.

By holding onto pain, fear, and other forms of negative energy, you are actively sabotaging your mindset and damaging your ability to enjoy your life. Let go. Let it all go. Those thoughts aren't serving you and you know it. You can feel the anxiety they create. It's wearing you down. But the good news is that it doesn't need to be that way. You can let go. The choice is yours.

The infinite power around you and within you cannot be tied to anything. There are no set boundaries to what you can be. Let go of the perception that you are tied to things. Expand your life. There are no limitations or boundaries around you.

Everything is happening perfectly.

Celebrate Small Wins Every Day

You must pat yourself on the back and congratulate yourself every day. You need to encourage and love yourself.

Celebrate small wins every day. Compliment yourself every day.

You are loved

as you are.

Be you.

You are enough.

Summary: You Are Enough

1) Ego is a delusion that you are not enough. You must get out of your delusion.

2) You are enough when you are authentic.

3) Perfection stops you from becoming who you are meant to become. Don't get stuck with perfection.

4) The past is past. Mistakes happen. That's called living. Keep moving forward.

5) Don't judge yourself or others. Accept others exactly as they are.

Homework

Pat yourself on the back and congratulate yourself. Continue this practice for the next 10 days.

YOU ARE
MEANT
FOR MORE

Chapter 9

YOU HAVE A BIGGER PURPOSE

There is an inner knowing inside you. In your gut, you know your path to your best life. You don't need to wait to get reinforcement from others when insights come to you. Act on them.

Suppose you tell a friend that you want to do something new, and they tell you that it's a bad idea. When you do nothing about it, based on their advice, you have an easy excuse to blame someone else for advising against it.

But why are you taking their advice? They don't know your path. Your path is yours. Everyone has their own path to meaning and growth. Follow your path. There will be detours in the road ahead; adjust, but don't give up. Keep adjusting until you can follow it confidently. Traipsing other people's paths will not give you fulfilment.

Your path is yours alone. Believe in it.

What do you want in life? Think about the big picture. Write it down. Don't ask how it will happen.

Don't make yourself small to make other people feel more comfortable. When you think small, you start looking for things that make you feel small. If you say, "*I am too old for this*," then you will find things to make you feel old. Your body will adjust to your emotional state and you will begin feeling older.

If your path is not one anyone around you has taken, you may feel afraid and alone. Although you know in your gut this is the right path for you, because others around you have not taken this path, they may discourage you, judge you, or encourage you to take another path instead.

Don't ask for permission from other people. The only permission you need in life is your own. Give *yourself* permission. Trust your instincts. Follow your intuition. There are no mistakes in life; it is *your* journey.

When you move according to your own intuition, you will have a greater momentum than if you follow someone else's path.

Surround yourself with like-minded people. Can you find a role model who's followed the path you also want to take? If there are people you admire, whether you know them personally or not, it is because the thing that you admire about them is something that you already are or want to become. You only recognize in others that which you are yourself.

If you have no role models to follow, you must widen your network. You can find role models by reading. If somebody has faced similar challenges, read their books, and find out how they overcame them. What beliefs did they have to shift to overcome their obstacles? Have the confidence to be vulnerable enough to try something new. Don't be afraid to fail. When things don't work, adjust and change. Start small. Continue to learn and grow. Don't give up.

When you are focused on a single goal, you can produce the desired results. When your focus is directed haphazardly, you cannot produce effective results. Become obsessed with how you want your life to be. Design it. Don't leave it to chance.

You Are Meant for More

We all have things we are good at. No one is less than the other and no one is more than the other. The higher power always gives you something to value. We are all equal, but you don't need to live your life the same way as others. We can appreciate and enjoy our differences. Nothing is missing from your life. You have things within you that truly fulfil you. If you want more, go and get it. Do more of the things that you love, the things that inspire you. You can choose this moment to live in your natural flow state with a belief that all things are possible for you, and begin taking small steps towards your best life.

There is a next level up for you. You are meant for more. Take the path that gives you growth. Beauty surrounds you. There are miracles around you. You are here for a reason.

Your path

is yours alone.

Own your path.

Believe in it.

Summary: You Have a Bigger Purpose

1) In your gut, you know the path to your best life. There is an inner knowing.

2) Own your path to your best life.

3) It is unfair to ask other people about your path to your best life. They don't understand your path.

4) When you are focused on a single goal, you can produce the desired results.

5) Take the path that gives you growth.

Homework

What do you want in life? How do you feel when you are doing things that are in line with your path?

Write down one paragraph on it.

Chapter 10

YOUR IDENTITY

Words that you use to identify yourself are powerful.

"I am" are the most powerful words you can use in your day-to-day life because you become what your "I am" is.

To use this to your advantage, you must become aware of the words you are using to describe yourself. Using empowering "I am" statements makes you feel good, grows your confidence, and makes you feel appreciated and energized. Empowering "I am" statements might include:

"I am a creative person."

"I am helpful."

"I am fit."

"I am smart."

"I am a great mother."

"I am the type of person who makes people laugh."

"I am beautiful."

"I am young and vibrant."

"I am cheerful."

"I am confident."

"I am an expert."

"I am resourceful."

"I am a great gardener."

"I am professional."

Using disempowering statements drains your energy. Disempowering "I am" statements include:

"I am an idiot."

"I am not attractive."

"I am a procrastinator."

"I am addicted to sugar."

"I am useless."

"I am old."

"I am sick."

"I am a worrier."

"I am a smoker."

"I am a bad person."

"I am not a good communicator."

"I am weak."

Change your disempowering "I am" statements to empowering statements.

Change your *"I am old."* to *"I am young and vibrant."* When you identify yourself with the statement, *"I am young and vibrant,"* your mentality will change your everyday life. You will want to exercise more and become more involved in activities. You will feel more energized because of it.

The "I am" statements that you use make a difference to how you feel at any given moment. Repeat these empowering statements with absolute certainty while moving your body. These are also your affirmations.

You can even name yourself with a new identity that fits your new state. *"I am unstoppable Alexis."* *"I am resourceful Justin."* *"I am Queen Bee."* Have fun with this!

You can call on this identity when you are in a negative frame of mind or need to make a decision, making it easy to act as though you are this new identity.

Use your "I am" statements consciously and carefully.

You become your "I am."

You become

your

"I am"

Summary: Your Identity

1) Words that you use to identify yourself are powerful.

2) "I am" is the most powerful phrase you can use to identify yourself.

3) You become your "I am."

4) Using empowering "I am" statements make you feel good, grow your confidence, feel appreciated, and energized.

5) You can even name yourself with a new identity that fits your new state.

Homework

Think of five "I am" words that you use regularly to describe yourself. Are they empowering or disempowering you? If they are disempowering you, change them.

Chapter 11

GIVING

Growth and contribution are spiritual needs. You feel alive when you are growing and contributing. It gives you a sense of purpose. How can you give more? How can you be more?

A lot of things in life are free to give. Giving a stranger a smile. Giving a compliment. Saying thank you when you receive a compliment. Listening and seeking to understand other people's views and opinions. Accepting others as they are. Loving and appreciating others. Doing random acts of kindness. Donating your time to a local charity. Helping someone in a time of need. Preparing a fantastic meal for your family and friends. Giving encouragement. Giving out good thoughts. Giving prayers. Providing your expertise. Performing chores for an elderly person. Offering to babysit kids. Planting a tree. Campaigning for a cause you believe in.

Compassion

The path to true service runs straight through compassion. When you have a high level of compassion for others, you are motivated to help to meet their needs. The possibilities for your personal growth and the value that you can contribute to the world are endless once you put compassion at the center of everything that you do. Of course, it is easy enough to say, "Find compassion." Actually doing it is another matter entirely.

How do you feel compassion? A good start is to focus on gratitude. Put some conscious effort toward reminding yourself when you ought to be thankful for something. When someone does something for you, when the weather is nice, when you receive a gift, remind yourself to embody gratitude. By finding gratitude, compassion will flow a lot more easily.

Cheerleader

Cheerleading is about actively and openly championing others' work. Be a cheerleader for others. Don't wait for others to show their support for you before you do so for them. When you believe in someone else, let them know! Help them have fun. It makes them feel appreciated.

Giving

Giving is receiving. You feel great when you give. Continue to give either your time or by other means to help individuals, communities, and the rest of the world. The secret to true happiness is giving.

The secret

to true happiness

is giving.

Summary: Giving

1) Growth and contribution are spiritual needs.

2) A lot of things in life are free to give.

3) The path to true service runs straight through compassion.

4) Be a cheerleader for others.

5) The secret to true happiness is giving.

Homework

Do a random act of kindness today.

KEEP THE
MOMENTUM

Chapter 12

KEEP MOVING FORWARD

U nexpected challenges will happen. Accidents, health issues, the loss of loved ones, relationship breakups, career loss. This is part of life. Sometimes it can help to think of these events as chapters. Your life has many chapters. You must turn the page to get to the next chapter in your life. It is about moving forward with purpose.

Embrace the unknown. When life is going well, everything may seem ordered, perhaps like nothing will ever go wrong again. But there will be difficult times in your future when you will have a loss of direction for whatever reason. In these difficult times, accept the unknown and embrace it. Life is happening exactly as it is meant to happen.

Learn from the past, but don't remain there. Focus on where you want to go.

Keep moving forward.

It's your life. You are in the driver's seat.

Fear

Fear is an unpleasant strong emotion that you have when you are in danger, when you feel bad things might happen to you, or when a particular thing frightens you. Fear is a state of mind.

Fear is a voice filling your head with negative thoughts. Fearful thoughts can include worry about illness, rejection, loneliness, looking foolish, or of accidents occurring.

Listening to this voice in your head keeps you stuck in dissatisfying situations, and will keep you experiencing the negative emotions. This voice of fear is sometimes called the chatterbox because it incessantly talks to you when you are fearful. Fearful thoughts include, "*You made a terrible mistake,*" "*You can't do it,*" "*You don't know anything,*" "*Nobody cares about you,*" "*Your life is over,*" and "*You will never be happy again.*"

You need to remove the power the fearful voice has over you. First, you will need to become aware of it. Consciously repeat positive affirmations. Then, listen to your inner voice, which will guide you.

You may say there is pain in your life. What is pain anyway? Give another meaning to this pain. Perhaps it is an opportunity to grow. Sometimes you spend precious time reliving pain that happened to you in childhood, or even pain that you only witnessed, because it happened to your loved ones and affected you. You may think this is being a loving soul because you care about the loved one that was in pain, but real love starts with yourself. Love yourself first. That means you must take care of yourself ahead of other people. Are you experiencing joy, peace, appreciation? When was the last time you really laughed? There is nothing stopping you from enjoying your life in this moment.

Don't numb yourself with outside stimulants. That might work for a few hours, but you won't feel good afterwards because it is temporary. Numbing yourself doesn't solve your problems.

You have the power to redesign your life by becoming aware of your thoughts. Smile, and don't be upset if you notice that you have the same negative thoughts again and again. Celebrate because you are aware of them now, and can now work at changing them. You can continue on for a long time without knowing the damage the negative thoughts are doing to your body, your mental health, and your life. But when you become aware of these negative thoughts, you can question them and work to change them. Is there any truth to these thoughts or fears? If believing these thoughts makes you fearful, then change these thoughts to ones of gratitude instead.

What can your life become if you don't listen to these negative thoughts?

Little Things and the Big Things

Many things in our life are free. Nature is free. Get out and enjoy nature's beauty.

Look around you and notice things that are built for your convenience. Appreciate them.

Little things and the big things are the same because their size depends on the meaning you give them.

You make your world the way you want it to be.

Focus

If an area of your life is going well, it is because you have put your focus on that area. If an area is not going well, you may have pulled focus or have taken it for granted.

Energy flows where focus goes. Consciously choose where your focus goes.

Where do you want to go? What do you want? Don't focus on what you don't want. Focus on what you do want. Direct your mind to where you want to go.

Focus on the solution and not the problem. When you become aware of yourself focusing on the negative, redirect your focus to the positive.

Personal Development

I get my inspiration from reading other personal development books. I am so grateful to all the personal development authors who have shared their experiences, knowledge, and tools. I used to buy personal development books to read but now I love listening to audiobooks because I can listen while I am doing activities such as cooking, walking, and driving.

Some authors' messages resonate greatly with you. When you find those authors, pick one or two things from their teachings that you can incorporate in your life.

Keep Moving Forward

Who you are becoming while you follow the path to your best life is a process, not a destination. You must continue learning, growing, and developing. There is a next level for you. A life of meaning, fulfilment, joy, and freedom.

Keep moving forward.

Embrace the

Unknown.

Keep Moving

forward.

Summary: Keep Moving Forward

1) Your life has many chapters. You must turn the page to get to the next chapter in your life.

2) Quieten your voice of fear and listen to your inner voice, which will guide you.

3) Energy flows where focus goes. Consciously choose where your focus goes.

4) You must keep learning, growing, and developing. Embrace the unknown.

5) There is a next level for you. A life of meaning, fulfilment, joy, and freedom.

Homework

Spend some time outside enjoying nature.

Chapter 13

CREATE YOUR REALITY

You will have experiences as you go through life, and it's the way in which you experience them that makes the difference. The quality of your life is determined by the meaning that you give to your experiences. Don't be concerned about how other people are defining what you are going through. It is <u>your</u> experience.

All experiences are just a blank slate. There is no meaning attached to these experiences. You can choose what takes up space in your life and your mind.

The meaning you give to an experience or situation will determine the action, emotion and eventual outcome. Is this a crisis, or a life transformation? How you respond mentally, physically, and emotionally depends on how you interpret what is happening. If you consider it a crisis, you may suffer from anxiety, flashbacks, grief, denial, regret, numbness, dizziness, nausea, chills, sleeping concerns, headaches, and tiredness. Whereas if you consider it a life transformation, you may experience, wonder, joy, happiness, love, peace, excitement, pride, awe, optimism, courage, satisfaction, energy, and confidence.

If you believe "*your life is over*" because something you consider to be terrible has happened, then you will experience your life consistent with this belief. Your body and emotional well-being will automatically reflect these thoughts. If you believe that this moment is a life transforming moment, then you will manifest all the experiences consistent with a life transformation. Your experience in the present and the future is dependent on the meaning you give to your past experiences.

Have you ever examined your life and thought, "*Gosh, that experience was actually good for me. It made me grow. It made me the person I am today. If it was not for that experience, I would not be the same individual.*"

All experiences make you grow. You are the person you are today because of those experiences.

Search for all the ways that an experience has helped you to become who you are today. Every experience is an opportunity for you to grow to become a better person. Shift your mindset so that you are curious about your experiences instead of afraid of them.

There is no actual reality. There is only your perception of your reality. You create the meaning of your reality.

Creative Visualization

You create everything twice. Once in your mind and once in your life.

Visualization is a powerful tool. Visualization is the mental image of what you want to happen in your life.

Anything you visualize in your mind, you can achieve in life. The key to visualization is to create an image in your mind as if you already have that which you are trying to attain. When your mind believes you already have whatever you are imagining, when you feel emotions connected to the images you are visualizing, this will attract them into your life.

Creative visualization is a technique that is widely used by athletes to enhance their performance. They visualize reaching their goals, they see themselves attaining their goals, and they visualize the specifics of their every movement, their emotions, and their environment.

There is a big difference between fantasizing and visualization. Visualization is a conscious process of creating an image in your mind and believing it will happen. Fantasizing is daydreaming about something that you believe you cannot obtain.

You must be relaxed and focused when you are visualizing. The more specific the image you visualize, the quicker it will appear in your life. If you are finding it difficult to relax, try using a breathing technique. Inhale and exhale slowly and naturally. Do this a few times until you feel that your body is relaxed.

To help you prepare for visualization, you can also begin by thinking of exceptional moments in your life. This might be the birth of your child, getting a promotion at work, or meeting your spouse or your best friend. You might have been in a flow state in that moment. You might have been euphoric. Recalling these moments will make you feel joy, helping you to get into a state of happiness and be ready for visualization.

Affirmations combined with creative visualization are powerful in manifesting lasting change. Once you have written all your affirmations, you must visualize them. If your affirmation is "*I am healthy and I feel great*," then visualize how you are feeling right now when you are healthy and great. How is your body feeling? Feel every inch of your body. Feel your posture. The more specific your mental image is, the more powerful it is.

The quality of
your life is determined
by the meaning that you give to
your experiences.

Summary: Create Your Reality

1) The quality of your life is determined by the meaning that you give to your experiences.

2) There is no actual reality. There is only your perception of your reality.

3) Shift your mindset so that you are curious about your experiences instead of afraid of them.

4) When you visualize in your mind, you can achieve everything you are visualizing.

5) Affirmations combined with creative visualization are powerful tools for manifesting lasting change.

Homework

Think of a challenging experience in your past. Think of a new meaning you can give to this experience.

Chapter 14

DECIDE AND COMMIT

You no longer need to feel helpless when facing challenges or decisions. Decide and commit to taking action. If things don't work out, adjust. Don't be in a state of overwhelmed helplessness. When a decision needs to be made, make the decision and commit. If things don't work out, change it. Keep changing it until you get it exactly the way you want it. Do not spend a minute more being helpless. Helplessness does not serve you.

Decide, commit, and move forward.

What are the emotions that you want to feel right now? Start with that intention. Life is about making decisions, and decisions shape your life. There is no right or wrong decision. You can adjust and change your mind if this is not what you want. Making a decision is the first step. Commit. Act.

Making decisions is important when you are creating the life you want. Don't wait to make a perfect decision. Just make it. Once you make the decision, commit and take action.

Here are some examples of decisions:

Make a decision to stay in a positive state no matter what. Commit to this decision and when you are not doing it, become aware of it and change it.

Make a decision to create a new habit.

Make a decision to find things you are grateful for and write them down every day.

Make a decision to stop listening to the news.

Make a decision to start doing something in an area that you love.

Make a decision to surround yourself with positive people.

Make a decision to say no to things that don't serve you.

Make a decision to take care of your body.

Make a decision to listen more.

Make a decision to not judge other people.

Make a decision to spend quality time with loved ones.

Make a decision to do something new every day.

Make a decision to congratulate yourself for small wins.

Decide, commit, and move forward.

Make

a decision

to stay in a

positive state

no matter what.

Summary: Decide and Commit

1) Don't be helpless when facing challenges or decisions.

2) Decide and commit to taking action. If things don't work out, adjust.

3) Making a decision is the first step.

4) There is no right or wrong decision. You can adjust and change your mind if it is not what you want.

5) Decide, commit, and move forward.

Homework

What are two decisions you are making today that you will commit and take action on?

Write them down now.

Chapter 15

GRATITUDE PRACTICE

G ratitude is a feeling of appreciation for what one has. Cultivating an attitude of gratitude yields many benefits, physical, mental, and spiritual. Feeling gratitude in the present moment makes you happier, more relaxed, and improves your overall health and well-being.

Gratitude is about focusing on what you have rather than what you are missing in your life. When you focus on what you have, you build on that foundation. Your energy will soar when you concentrate on what you already have rather than what is missing in your life.

You are meant to live your life in a state of curiosity, excitement, appreciation, and joy. I call this a "gratitude state of mind," or gratitude practice.

A person experiencing gratitude feels a sense of joy and abundance in their life. They also feel more connected with other people and have increased energy.

Give Thanks for Everything

Gratitude doesn't just have to be about big things. You can be thankful for simple things such as enjoying a meal or walking around your neighborhood or appreciating nature. There is always something that you can be grateful for in your life. The end goal is about appreciating the things around you rather than taking them for granted.

Thank your possessions for serving you daily. Bed, cooker, toothbrush, clothes, cellphone, car, water, electricity, the air we breathe, the food we eat, the internet that allows us to work from home. All these things you take for granted. Yet everything is serving you beautifully.

Thank someone or compliment someone every day. Make sure you find a real reason to thank someone rather than a superficial one. Thank them, and don't expect anything from that person. Simply be thankful.

Give thanks for your daily experiences as well. Be aware of your surroundings. Notice the small things.

Small things can turn into big things if you notice them and start to appreciate them. Become aware, without judgment, of your emotions throughout your day. Everything is happening perfectly in this moment.

Write Them Down

If there is one piece of advice that I wish I could spread widely, it is this–writing down the things that you are grateful for really does work.

Have you ever done a regular activity that made you realize that you have been slowly changing as a result? You may not have realized it then, but after a while, you started to notice the difference in yourself. That is how I've come to feel about gratitude practice. I show up consistently. I write down five things I am grateful for every day. I sometimes read back the gratitude entries I have written over the years and I see the person I was then and the person I am now. I am much calmer and happier today because of this intentional practice.

Make it a ritual to write down things you are grateful for every day. Write them down in a gratitude journal or a notebook. When you know that you are going to write things down you are grateful for, you will start to look for things to be grateful for when you are going about your day. You are stacking things that you are grateful for and you will feel great during the day.

Your mind will filter only things that you want to enter your life when you start writing things down. You're looking for these wonderful things to write in your journal or notebook that you are appreciating. You're will start to feel great throughout your day.

Writing down things you are grateful for is more effective than merely thinking or saying them. It helps you focus on important things. You can also read and re-read what you have written down.

Gratitude is the foundation of your life. It is the foundation of what could be possible for you to live and lead your best life. Write down things you are grateful for every day. Start with small and everyday things.

Writing down what you are grateful for is an intentional practice. You look for things to have gratitude for and then write them down.

Cultivating an attitude of gratitude yields many benefits: physical, mental, and spiritual.

Summary: Gratitude Practice

1) Cultivating an attitude of gratitude yields many benefits: physical, mental, and spiritual.

2) Gratitude is about focusing on what you have rather than what you are missing

in your life.

3) Gratitude doesn't just have to be about the big things.

4) Thank everything for serving you daily.

5) Make it a ritual to write down things you are grateful for every day.

Homework

Write down five things you are grateful for today in a journal or notebook. Continue this practice.

CONCLUSION

This book is designed for you to become aware of how your thoughts, emotions, beliefs, and the statements you use shape your life.

Make sure you complete all the homework in this book. If you have missed an exercise, go back and do them now. Knowledge is not enough. You need to apply these tools to your life. Come back and do these exercises at least once a year as you continue on the journey of your best life.

Anytime you have negative thoughts, the first step is to become aware of them. Becoming aware of them is already a win. The state you are in influences the statements you are repeating to yourself which eventually become your beliefs. Your beliefs are self-fulfilling. When you believe something, you also manifest it. You receive what you believe. Therefore, you must question and investigate every negative belief you hold. You have the choice to consciously change your belief or state of mind anytime you want, and you do it by repeating positive affirmations. When you think and say positive affirmations, it makes you feel calm, confident, energized, and good inside.

Audit and evaluate your life. What areas are going well for you right now? What could make it even better? What areas need the most work? What are the gaps between where you are right now and where you want to be? Become clear on why you need to make the improvements. Investigate and question the beliefs in the areas that are holding you back. Begin making small shifts to move forward to where you want to be.

Surround yourself with positive people who challenge, encourage and support you. Become aware when there is negativity around you. By not joining them, you will protect your peace and confidence. Who you surround yourself with is who you become.

Audit your time. Say no to things that don't benefit you. Schedule and block time to spend on people you want to and doing things that you enjoy and love.

Self-care is your responsibility. You give love to yourself and others when you take care of your mind and body. Enjoy every minute of your life. Don't postpone your happiness. Design a morning routine that empowers you for the day.

Ego is the delusion that you are not enough. Be you. You are enough when you are authentic. Regrets happen, so don't waste time wishing your past was different. The past is past. Don't judge yourself or others. Let go of pain, fear, and other forms of negative energy. Celebrate small wins every day.

You are meant for more. There is an inner knowing inside you. You know your path to your best life, a life of joy, fulfilment, and freedom. Your path is yours alone. Don't ask for permission from other people to follow your path. Believe in it and permit yourself to follow a path of your own choosing. It is your journey, after all.

Words you use to identify yourself are powerful. Who are you really? Use empowering "I am" statements to describe yourself. Use your "I am" words consciously and carefully. You become your "I am."

Growth and contribution are spiritual needs. You feel alive when you are growing and contributing to others. It gives you a sense of purpose. The secret to true happiness is giving.

There is a next level for you. Keep moving forward with momentum. Energy flows where focus goes. Consciously choose where your focus goes.

Unexpected challenges are going to happen to you. The quality of your life is determined by the meaning that you give to your experiences. It is your experience. Embrace the unknown. It is about moving forward with purpose. There is no actual reality, only your perception of reality.

Don't wait to make a perfect decision. Just make it. Once you make the decision, commit and take action. An important decision you can make is to decide and commit to living in a positive state no matter what.

Cultivating a daily intentional gratitude practice helps you appreciate what you have rather than focusing on what you are missing in your life. Your gratitude must be directed towards everything in your life. It is the foundation of your life and is integral to all your experiences. Feeling gratitude makes you happier and more relaxed and improves your overall health and well-being. Make it a ritual to write down things you are grateful for every day. You'll be looking for these wonderful things that you will appreciate and write down, making you feel good throughout your day.

What is my belief in this area? What is my state of mind right now?

Become aware and ask yourself these questions whenever you need to make a decision.

With a positive belief and state of mind, you can shape your life in a way that truly fulfills you and empowers you to live your best life.

Thank you. I love you.

OTHER BOOKS
by Brenda Nathan

The One-Minute
Gratitude Journal

100 Popular Gratitude
and Motivational Quotes

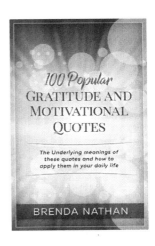

Visit website: www.brendanathanbooks.com

ACKNOWLEDGEMENTS

I would like to acknowledge and thank Oprah Winfrey, Tony Robbins, Wayne Dyer and Louise Hay.

NOTES

NOTES

NOTES

NOTES

Manufactured by Amazon.ca
Bolton, ON